DISTANT CLOSE

❖

WILL DAUNT

❖

Belfast
LAPWING

Published by Lapwing Publications
c/o 1, Ballysillan Drive
Belfast BT14 8HQ
Lapwing.poetry@ntlworld.com
http://www.freewebs.com/lapwingpoetry/

Copyright © Will Daunt 2008

All rights reserved

The author has asserted her/his right under Section 77
of the Copyright, Design and Patents Act 1988
to be identified as the author of this work.

British Library Cataloguing in Publication Data.
A catalogue record for this book is available from
the British Library.

Since before 1632
The Greig sept of the MacGregor Clan
Has been printing and binding books

All Lapwing Publications are
Hand-printed and Hand-bound in Belfast
Set in Times New Roman at the Winepress

ISBN 978-1-905425-73-0

ACKNOWLEDGEMENTS

Thanks to the editors of the following for publishing some of these poems:
Bard; Curlew; Envoi; Iota;
Poetry Cornwall; Poetry Monthly;
Pulsar; Time Haiku

Also by Will Daunt

Lancashire Working
Running Out Of England
The Good Is Abroad

CONTENTS

TOWERING SIDEWAYS	7
HILL-DOG	8
KIND INVASIONS	9
JULY, 2006	10
JULY, 2007	11
WIDENING GOLF	12
STRANGLED BLACKBIRD	13
SPRING LEAVES SKIPTON	14
THIRTY YEARS	15
SURREY AFFAIRS	16
CORNWALLS CONVERGE	17
SHARKS AT STAFFA	18
SHEEP CRAIG, FAIR ISLE	19
TRIG POINT	20
LAST CROFT ON EARTH	21
SILENT ISLAND	22
STIRLING EFFORTS	23
WHERE CAITHNESS ENDS	24
LOST CROSSING	25
DUTCH-DYKES	26
SKY-SCRAPING STRAND	27
OTHER COUPLES	28
AT THE EDGE OF CENTER PARCS	29
LANCASHIRE'S LAWNMOWERS	30
SKETCHED ON THE LAST TRAIN	31
LONDON SUNDAYS	32
HIS LITTLE LIFE	33
GO, & THEN RETURN	34
WET TENT	35
MAY AGAIN	36
LOVERSHOT	37
OCCASIONAL MOBILE GOLD	38
ANOTHER PLACE	39
FUTURE EARFUL	40
GROWING YOUNG	41
26/ 7/ 06	42

DISTANT CLOSE 43

Some Secret English Homes

    1a – 1e: The Flats 45
    3: Station Villas 46
    5: Unsemi-detached 47
    7: Political Hiccoughs 48
    9: Stationary Terrace 49
    11: Best Forgotten 50
    13a: Aviary 51
    13b: Hutch 52
    13c: Kennel 53
    13d: Run 54
    12: Good Grief 55
    10: At Home In Her Prison 56
    8: The Cottage That Wasn't 57
    6: Rocky 58
    4: Withdraw and Fade 59
    2: Coldfish 60

REVIEWS 61

For Caroline, Tom and Francis

TOWERING SIDEWAYS

The world is a dune of gulfs,
as flat as seas can lie:
great greasy treasure, wide,
and starting here, at Southport.

A subtle, slender ladder
propped against a sand-spume
of the mind, and sepia-
slow, it replays how we played.

Like an iron, sad idea
it peers past Blackpool's
steel needle, scans the downward
slide to Liverpool's free Graces.

Plodding poles across the sand
hold old and muddle-aged
above the slicks, or waves
like dim and grimmer rigs.

Some little shelter lodges
on a forward ledge, leans
speechlessly and south enough
to glimpse the mountain shade.

Find any world's end
or walk the planks of Southport.
They're primed to cast land out
beyond the sea. Journey there.

Distant Close

HILL-DOG
Conwy Valley

Old road, faint rain,
the seamy beams of sunless afternoon.
Scarp under calves.

Flat out and up,
that platitude of beauty
wrapped by duty,

at the lost house,
comes bounded kindred sprinting,
harried by barks:

spry-terrier.
Trotting off, lost up-and-over
yaps in the fold

and straddles lanes
where trees leave hill–high fences.
Beast's released.

Flustered flock
run sagging and roughed-up
off side-hills, off

rocky bog-side,
fall under a lolloping hunter
hound-dogged

bust, fumbling
with fleece-in-the-reeds,
like pine-lines

lost on contours.
Fifteen minute moments
flabbergast

by running, wild:
what petty beasts pull off
on mammoth hills.

KIND INVASIONS

The best of summer grows perversely
where we'd like to walk, and cannot.

Take the nettle, strung and livid,
sprung and lurking by each wood-path

or the overgrowth of briar,
runted rose and bloody berry.

Waive these binding weeds, which run
like rigging with their wispy pennants

twisted tight round dock and laurel,
either prone to wilt, unwanted.

Ditch your doubts of burr and thicket,
up the shrinking paths of summer.

Let their plain and prickly cordons,
impregnate the beaten track.

Distant Close

JULY, 2006

Those days unpicked the days
when roads were molten, smelt like flesh

and wizened stuff fell out of trees.
Home-timbers swelled and shrank as tides
in far, imagined seas

and many drew their own equator.
Undogs rolled in hard-caught shade
where hoses snaked about

and coarse lawns grilled to tinder.
Evenings stalked tough afternoons
becoming homes of languid fun

where offices were gardens, and
likewise, air-conditioned lives
turned up the dial, cooled down

and turned it higher. Always higher.

JULY, 2007

That rain dissolved our maps
and weeks were fused, like mercury

as every soiled surface gleamed.
Dark gutters bulged and bunged as tides
invaded thoroughfares

and flowers drowned in shiver-beds.
Unsung birds forgot the pitch
and point of serenading

while weeds waved loose and lengthily.
Translucent dawn took many days
and chocolate lakes slopped crops,

emulsifying into sludge.
Meanwhile, gangs of ruddy flab
filled up their baths, plunged in

and ran more water. Ran it hotter.

WIDENING GOLF

There are two vast crabs
in abandoned fields by the by pass.
Before dawn, you'll see
black Lancashire loam in their pincers.

Where darkness ends,
there's a murky pool for them to stalk
and flitting pairs of light
eye up the boundary, crawling.

Though undetected
by drivers' eyes
and undisturbed, they lurch
between these tees and stodgy bunkers.

There's an energy
in digging for pleasure
and empty, latent hills
throw backward shadows eastwardly.

In fact, the pastel scene
has shaded several parishes,
above this upturned earth
which hides the seed of former farms.

It's where many aim:
a drive that carves our country out
and lawns spread, ripe for auction.
A grub-house. Holes. Gas guzzlers. Holes.

STRANGLED BLACKBIRD

Funny, how we do what's best
without expecting something worse.

Stupid, how we thought it best
to net the currant canopy
and peg it to the fertile floor.
Early trees were full of nests.
Crazy, when you think of it
that all that fruit (we'd never eat)
required such a safety gauze
to help it wilt and wither.

Stranger, on that sparkled day
to come upon a death we'd bred
enmeshed among the berries:
how he clung, in love (not luck)
to that paradise of food
where an unplanned, instant trap
tourniqueted his slender neck.

Funny, how we grow what's best
for us, and leave the Earth to chance.
He's buried where our foxgloves lurk.

SPRING LEAVES SKIPTON

breathe in: broad meadows
and outcrops sprout, like reconceived
high, living springs

Dale
blown gloss of bluebell
in bark-brown and wilderness
livid with garlic

Verge
buttercup bolsters
the red bed of hawthorn
which cow parsley pillows

Bed
laburnum shudders
lilacs shrivel, wallflowers
fall, while roses rise

Treeline
late-leafing beck-birch
or roots of moist sessile oak
hugging the rubble

Ever-grief
why, after winter,
these flimsy survivors,
these tendrils and splinters?

THIRTY YEARS
Copthorne

A drive home is the road to doubt,
and even when reluctant signs
correct the way-to-go, a steady
compass grips your every turn
on dawn-swept roads, from a blindside
of glare in sudden sun.

                Like that time
when the early-shores ferry was prompt
and a day slunk away like uncoiled rope.
Kids slept through the Sussex border,
while downland, like shadow, leant
on some half-smothered, thirty year
odd memory: that obsolete home
in an over-spilt village. 'Just a quick look'.

By the time you'd manœuvred the lanes
and closes, gulped at a clutch of fields (fallen
into housing) each was awake. 'Dad, why
are we here? I'm tired. I'm thirsty. Let's …'
And, at that, you vaguely snapped,
nagged by what should have come back
like longing for games in that garden's shade.

Which wasn't there. The house slept, appended
at several angles: the cauterized thicket,
a vast and aimless patio, brash gates
and clematis, hanging at random.
That happy gap of lawn had been
(as you knew when you'd remembered)
sold off, cut down and leveled,
shored up and shoved off, like a lattice
landscape, marked out and ravaged
by builders.

                Self-preservation
meant you said, 'Those houses must be new.
Who could have put them there?'

SURREY AFFAIRS

Impressions blotched at midge-time re-appear.
They wade through pools, impregnate sand,
shrug showers from umbrellas;

from collars down the sopping heath
they spot how clouds appear to weep
make loveliness in gorse;

in heaving sweeps of heather beds
the adder slithers longingly
and nightjars taint the dusk;

artillery recalls a pang,
like that imagined range of hills
and supple, unstroked thighs.

If only this lost heath of pines,
of pressed and printed country-seeds
and their bright facsimiles

could re-connect a satin sun
with mundane moments of the love
that gathers here in brackish glades.

CORNWALLS CONVERGE

A hedge is not a hedge
but some fraternal rat race -
hawthorn in bracken, oak
and gorse, sewn with renegade rose.

The beach is not the beach
but a mortar bowl of glass, shell,
infinite shapes of marble, wood
and dead and eddied shards of how we live.

A wood is not a wood
but undergreen and overgrowth
or even a canopy stack
of croaking rook and jackdaw squawks.

The sky is not the sky
and doesn't level orangely
or shrivel into drizzle hills
without appearing otherwise, nearby.

A river's not a tide
or cliff a precipice, or field
a feeble tilt at life, or travel
less than what we thought at home, inspired.

A place is not its name,
hence: Indian Queens, Victoria,
London Apprentice, Bugle, Sticker,
Sweetshouse, Puddle or Bowling Green.

Distant Close

SHARKS AT STAFFA

Beyond Iona, and it seems
as final as a happy grave
or harmony, besieged by blue
tectonic pleats of sea.

Beneath the mists and massive
in the gravity of Mull,
a satellite obtrudes,
a star that cooled too soon.

Before those honeycombs of there
prod oddly out of tiny tides,
your stubby launch will pause
and circle, like a decoy, coy

beside its blunt arrival.
Through a mesh of seaweed-surf,
little less than surging luck
jolts you up the jetty's hint.

Behind this rust and bitumen,
the specious views of basalt
bar each cave and duty spot
and memory snaps, vaguely.

Below the hulking hull
and crag, two other grey, deep
slumberers, ape submarines
and soundlessly are basking past.

How good is it to seem like them,
indifferent and free to flow
down those broad undertows of cold
where rock and sea entwine, inter.

SHEEP CRAIG, FAIR ISLE

A lopped and brutish tumour,
adrift from its isthmus, uselessly.

A bog of clods on unseen scarp,
and veering, virile sweeps of turf.

A sighing islet, proud and lone.
A fort left off to tussle wind.

A crazy past, brave stringing up
of sheep in boats, to precipice.

A summer meadow, winter shelf,
or outpost of an older life.

A grazing, outside tidal rims
and slight inhabitation.

TRIG POINT
Colonsay

Gales

and where

to gawp but downwards.

Bracken landing, granite lurking.

Landscape tones like later sun, spilling.

Shaking heather. Breakers of weather, beached

on some lonely stones. Mountains of water spooling.

Brackland peat-haze, laid-back lochs. Sand expanding,

s   h   i   v   e   r   i   n   g   s   e   a .

LAST CROFT ON EARTH
Oronsay

An unclaimable, caught
by its halo of sands
and horizons at dawn.

Another expiry of road
in a buried bouquet
of iris and reed.

A pattern of rubble
and fragments of sash-frame
at home in the strand.

A surplus of stray-light
and salt and air,
or a rock-place

of closure, washed nightly
like paradise, blind
and aloof and unknown.

Distant Close

SILENT ISLAND

Where did the noise and ferry go?

Across the sound,
tandems, lorries, ordered trees
and cars laid out with waiting,

all alive and soundless.

And here, in small, stone ground
there's always nowhere neat to park,
no signposts, yet, like sentries
benches out-look
each secluded beach.

Under dented rocks,
occasional crags,
(some sprayed loud, like totems)
the splayed flock stands out, madly.

Who cycled out
and sat here first, and why?
Where did a love for lay-bys grow,
over mud-red shorelines?

Trip of a daytime, out of Glasgow:
many know this. Few discover.

STIRLING EFFORTS

Full-hardy fuschia
bloodily blooms and shudders
under mountain ash

while renegade writers
extrapolate emptiness,
calling it art.

Vistas of thistle
from granule to chasm
hold down a misty day

smudging ideas
across made up reminders
of unwritten verse.

And burns spread like veins
throughout arms of a landscape
where fresh mosses merge,

and voices diverge
like words in a wilderness -
grit fills the vacuum.

WHERE CAITHNESS ENDS

Each tide at Duncansby
whirls an index
round vague stacks

to clasp the inlets
for certainty.

Each harbour
(shacks and battered wall)
grips the surge
as bitterly as rigid hands
determined, and compressed
against the weathers.

Did I think of you
while squeals rose,
plumage plunged
and boats were easing into port?

Will Daunt

LOST CROSSING

Such ports are where
expiring summers close. Lax anglers
hurl a cast or catch
as far and finally as long-tossed buoys
or crusty, buried creels.
And causeways point the course
like quirks and curiosity
which run amuck along this shore.

Dull islanders leave Europe
on the swell of drowning pools.
Their walkways plummet waterwards
and ferry swathes pour up a froth,
of muddled love and loss

like autumn berthing.

Distant Close

DUTCH-DYKES

A gauze and grid which liquidly
drink up and penetrate the land.

A large percent of water-lanes
with slender verges, soiled shoals.

A needlework of nature, patched
by undressed trees and wisps of spring.

A net of winding tinder tracks
which fritter by opaque canals.

A way to launch yourself - or slump -
on lichen-stricken landing planks.

SKY-SCRAPING STRAND
Zandvoort

Like hooded gulls, or slick-backed crows,
some top-drawn, top-floor lovers sketch
a loud and lofty collage, doodle
lazily and guess each other's gaze.
Below, the cusp of insect strand
and saline bowl slops out and in.
Wave gnaws at beach, which sides with sky.

These are whispering shifts of land
and sunk savannahs, tower blights
in clotted, mud-wide reservoirs.
To rise above their fracture
leaves the coast remote, while sea,
that illusion of ending,
offers views without edges, or end.

OTHER COUPLES
Haarlem

To be with you and yet without
the soul of how we synchronize:
with art and food and sun, to crave
a flavour of being one, forever;
for that to gleam in Masters' oils
and hug the hedges' pungent curls;
to feel it under gables' light
where kerbs, like bullets, leave us lost.

Such escapades (within the breach
that not-being-parted ought to solve)
resemble love attached to chance:
so side-by-side, such time alone.

We could have spent that day apart, like this,
if we were other lovers, short of bliss.

AT THE EDGE OF CENTER PARCS

Upon a hill, where spruced-up families
thrust or plan collapse across the needles,
late ideas occur, of paradise -
a rash of smart stockades, leased and luxurious.

They cost another forest, where gruff trucks
ran aground in mud, or bust on tundra.
Ships slipped into ports, almost submerged
with unsung wombs of wood. Would that

they saved our dark, far out plantations
beyond the believable, oddly cold;
but here, in a million weekends there has been
some curious flirting with our future's future.

It grows at every English curve and close,
a cross-bred kind of eco-cabin, suave
and almost Swedish, warm and roomy,
imagined on the car-stack route from Preston.

It's a fortunate fold for the fauna,
or better, some shot from a guide book
with all the grainy background of a forest,
or Britain getting off, astride its mountains.

Sky-low shots and routes to this stockade
get taken and held up, frameless and cold-framed,
like a collaged nature, reserved, alone
and where we have it: all or nothing,

a passport to mid-life in the wild
with pioneer-heroes we'd love to be.
Security rules are simple: lock out guilt.
The silver-bellied Air Force will keep watch.

LANCASHIRE'S LAWNMOWERS

After vats of rain and assumptions of grey
through windscreen and troubled glazing, through this smear,
a shy and climbing arclight picks us out, and up
and colours sharpen, multiply and shock
in the din of nothing, out in blotted awfuls.

And whiffs of silence dry on the lacquered branch
or a light, distilling taste of undrenched chaff
returns to thermals, gilt in evaporation,
under new, inverted seas of choice and leaving
over the stiffened coat of what's alive.

And first, a blacker chunter from the shacks
as squads of petrol prams gob out
with rusty rotors, stripe and score a gash
in meadows, cut to the trace. Tanker or tug,
they creak and growl, nudged by fairer winds.

But soon the mob is spent. Here are others:
midges that mishit the million airs
and dragonfly-prisms - brilliant, brief,
while martins surf updrafts
and pipistrels dangle, eager to strafe.

SKETCHED ON THE LAST TRAIN

Here comes another pinhole, night-long, white incision. Gardens shine
and amber streets rack upwards and apart. We're carried awry
by long and babbled racket, as low as rattled flatulence.
We're softly knocked & rolled on well-greased steel,
ball bearings alive in a rut from where we've been.
Furtive mobiles name each destination,
while lines fold up their locals limbs.
The smudge of Runcorn wanes
and, as we nudge the Mersey,
kiosks close, sleepers sleep
a final camber sparkles -
west by west-of-north
- the missile misses,

q u i e t l y

i m p l o d e s

LONDON SUNDAYS

slight, tinny engines
like fireworks up thin streets,
like fiddle strings whining

sirens and ripples
distort, yell and rescue
a chaos of pain

a faked embrace: trains
above archways that rattle
the soot on to signs

more metal migrants
flock in a sequence, screech,
landing narrowly

a million listeners
sulk, caress or lie alone
above dark back yards

HIS LITTLE LIFE

Faint landing lights elapse upon each dark
and large disasters pass us as we sleep.
Are comets less for being far away,
while flashlights in the yard appear to creep?

We undertook a modest death today,
uncaged his empty hemisphere, and wept.
Why minor lives jar hearty strings, God knows,
like continents of sorrow, where they're kept.

GO, & THEN RETURN

Happiness hangs like blue cover of June
a comfort of friends and the skyshine seen.

Almost an orb of wide summer and wine
with an untimely day-late to sleep, outside in.

Lazy light happens and work-wounding heals
and lambent tunes waft within garden-gold walls.

A riper voice names how to dazzle a day.
'Your life has reached August. Some summer, so soon'.

WET TENT

… and blindly woke unknowing how he'd flopped there,
touched the canvas cavern arch while
here and now broke off from where and why

and sank that well-pegged craft in August dew
some docking made in tropics that he'd dreamt
and felt the syrup sponge on which they'd slept

gave in to all that didn't need undoing
let early breeze in spasms exhale damply
a sense of some close friend some way away

and understood some good in being lost
when missing from the trip-shape rules already
aged again, but saw the gap he'd learnt was large

Distant Close

MAY AGAIN
Sedbergh

an oak
bent-over, coarse
and propping
slopes prepared to burst
with heather, purple-pale
greater greenness
kaleidoscope rays
in dribbled windows
coal-cats siting
prey through showers
conifers flagging
frail and battered
buttercups sprayed
and lamb-loves-feeding
mosses bouncing,
rocks in bracken,
torrents off
by rash of daisy
ragged hawthorn
bursting verges
England away recovering itself
lines of sun on shale.

Will Daunt

LOVERSHOT

At any strand, awash with waves
massed cranks and waifs and wanderers
in love with how to be in love
depart the promenade, detach
to some post-ambled, sea-determined, disadvantage point.

They blink and plan a batch
of poses, snapped or half-revised
from mirrorville or album-slum.
So neatly done: attempted, warm
and digitally crafted, more yet less than what they ever quite desired.

OCCASIONAL MOBILE GOLD

In a crass and graceless place
watch for where half-couples chat
to screens and small machines.
Have they cleared their message box
and earned an empty in-tray, slipping up or out, unseen?

Are they fagged out on their breaks,
skirting shops and gossips' eyes
or texted out by loving?
These gorgeous ghosts, and yet ...
once in a mile, two smiles touch, unelectrically.

Will Daunt

ANOTHER PLACE
Crosby 2006

crushed runways of silt
sliding on their tiny slope
or infinite plinth

broad tidal plunge bath
overflowed at speed of sand
unplugged by moonlight

brown loners' outing
seeking shipwreck dusk and storm
stuck alone agog

another army
marches from the landward end
slow, bold or humble

FUTURE EARFUL

These ear-pods dangled
with demon tunes
came from where?

What in the weirdest
orb of melodies
whispers through?

Who warbled tons
of circuit-sparks
in mini-microchips,

and which enormous
sound was somehow
funnelled from their youth?

Why does it count
in the dream of things
when we sing, and somehow

define which key we're in?
Are pattering beats
the vertebrae of self?

Do sheer guitars
shear sheaves of dreariness
from unloved lives?

And keyboards:
do they polarize the black
and white inside?

And who is still in tune?

And who is playing safe?

GROWING YOUNG
For Keith Chandler

What, sixty? Pull the other one.
You've taught the young to hate the old
and shown the old the youth they'd lost,
while making teaching sharp and fun.

Get out of it! You, pensioned off?
Those Norfolk folk forgot to say,
'Oi, you, yes Poet-all, you there!
Don't even think of going west, or soft…'

26/ 7/ 06

… & when you glance behind you, see

the heather hills

our twenty years

like silhouettes of scenery

& past that happy foreground

light & shadow,

double-beauty,

leans the whole extent ahead

one landscaped independent land

of happiness & love

as far as lives

can gaze, from then & now

Will Daunt

DISTANT CLOSE

Some Secret English Homes

Distant Close

1a – 1e: The Flats

There is a space in your dreams where a sky of lights shines
and a temperate breeze puts the scene in its place
but no-one revives.

There's a couple of lives scudding under the blue;
how neon their ceilings, how dated their floors
halogenically numb.

This is some block of flops shovelled out of a Blitz
like a scream-home, a hut above, flat-broken
skyline of space.

From the base of some fortunate, disparate view
look where the tenants gawp, over the rift
raised here to leave

and bunged in the basement are other ways round,
where, without hope (being deep and distracted)
top floors appeal.

Distant Close

3: Station Villas

To start with, I come to an end. Here are three sleek
and crimson walls, a hundred years apart.
This half is the start of my happenstance,
its drapes drawn, gaping and amber, all evening.
This launching-part for umpteen other homes
transcends a new and retro-lamp-lit route.
My chimney's abreast of fine courses of fiction,
abutting the gritty brick, cover-coded
from Penguin orange to Wisden sand.
If only this library rewrote the tale, shaping
some damaged recovery room, making luck
where brazen bands play, sadly. No such love:
my rooms are spare, ruddy, sparse and replete
or stung with nameless placards, nice designs
in interior milieux , more clutter than culture
soft-bogus postcards and soft-torn art.
I'd be pleased to please neighbours if-and-when
some other jumps inside my clutch of tunes.

5: Unsemi-detached

Neighbours! Hate-em-or-leave-em, they're all a sham.
Take our stablemate: take him and heave him
somewhere beyond where the refuse tip stinks.
Nothing round here's for real, see for yourself –
we're self-made women, well stung men, hamper-
ed by little but little lives. Like next door's.
God, he's drabber than school – that far back
music at all hours, long songs with desperate wordshows
shuddered with bass, and desperate drumming.
Being-yourself, being heavy on the self. How we'd
hate to be anything less, or slide out of these rituals
of playing at being six versions of who-you're-not.
In an evening with us, you'd learn to be how
and – well, maybe, what - somehow you're scared
to become. We live by the instant - brash, bad
and plastic, and that, for a start, will do, you-know?

Do little, live well. Love leaving the bore of life
to settle up late in a different, disposable day.

7: Political Hiccoughs

'Praise the bored for we have found
a library of means to name ourselves.
Ditto, this house of nil dispute
and happiness ducked for fear of offence.

'And thanks to one and nil for all
our slipshod, misshaped, smug morale,
dressed down as morals. Laud the beard,
for it hath barred the truth from being heard.

'God, to have gods on your side ...
whether slower-than-thou or sanitized ,
this smug belief is self-insured
or frigid, bored and over-ruled and sure.

'Our creed would lie unneeded,
if only we found neighbours, good and true'.

9: Stationary Terrace

We're safe in our hand-me-downs. Hand over that album
and help to re-recall again - how nothing's changed.
This is the house that settled back into a home
which no-one dreamt would be our long-loved own.
It should never have caught three sisters. Yet - look here -
old crockery set in our sideboard, wry and dry.

One of us once was a leisurely-length of leather,
rainbowed scarves, always on or near the groove
and grace even rummaged a hand in other drawers:
costumes were borrowed, hangers wrapped. We hid and hung
around for forty years. Mimicking women,
we watched for lovers' outlines, through the privet.
.
Each week, we'd've died to've had more outings planned.
Our own little, outcast sisterhood: chosen, ruled.

11: Best Forgotten

You're vague, when I look curious and sigh,
'Remember nostalgia?'

and you talk of what's left, how long it might work
and what hasn't managed to happen,

whether somehow this liquid and limp appeal
might be better repackaged

with something less tangible, somebody new
out there in an untested future

in equal, familiar, unfocused distress
to this, which has split one from two.

What was it you said that we shouldn't have been?
Do you reckon you've won?

I think it was you - it might have been me -
who said, 'And what's thirty years?'

13a: Aviary

Bird song? I'll give you bird song
'til your sick of twittering. Look -
much better, listen. I've reversed
this cage called home, culled half
the usual clutter, made each room
a gaping prison. Moved outside
and made a bird-world happen.
For why? Well, just to stuff your ways
and therefores, put your tidy kinds
of mind back in their tiny drawers,
while in my open lair, the wings
of change are one distended
family, taking off. Almost.

13b: Hutch

Once outside, you're done for.
Hold hope and flight against
the wiry life you trimmed
down to a shoe-box. Live apart
and watch messes through a mesh.
Chafe your shell against the trap-
door, warped by winter squalls.
No fun's coming to let you out.
No different day will feed you,
other than that when kids escape
within the barricades.
What then - enticement,
warmth, or more insipid food?

13c: Kennel

My masters' trust and love
is just enough to chain me here
and terrify the neighbours.
They tried the yard, but events
overtook the jaunt they'd planned
at an amble. I'd love a lease
in the wheel-world, driven out
and parked almost casually,
up some open close. Howling
at the gawping door, who knows
who's hounded, who's the hound?
Hauling myself back, who knows
where I'll lollop, after dusk?

13d: Run

Up/down, about/ along, like
a preposition on wheels, like
a proposition in prison, like
a night after day release, like
realising it's unreal, like
lying to be believed, like
leaving before you've arrived, like
vying for no-one's acclaim, like
proving there's nothing to show, like
showing your shadow the way, like
running away on the spot, like
being unlike and unliked, like
being fenced into a life.

12: Good Grief

I thought that none could make me trip so soon
(because her death was still a far-fetched fact)
but you were right about when I'd been wrong
(in skulking from the great and late beyond).

She hasn't left enough and in that gap
(which you had warned could pierce or shatter us)
I've loved the cruel company of this
(while you've hogged all the love that feeds the hurt).

Sometimes the space of being left is plain
(and somehow sweet and tinted words disperse)
but what is worse is watching others bloom
(with all the vivid elegance of loss).

Was that a spouse or sibling, lover, child,
or just the seed of grief in all of us?

Distant Close

10: At Home In Her Prison

This is another's fortress, better be sure.
You can't be yourself and the door frames yawn
with a drab, imagined wealth. Your pocket drains
before the parquet's sheen has bought your eye.

To have slobbed and slipped through here, by God,
with that dirty warmth of breathing traffic -
what a hope! Yet others in the Close go on
about their distant business, like some book.

That could be decent history, when and if,
but family flits like dolls throughout this house
a residue of how we might have lived.
All very well when not at one with hell

when not an unloved, lovely prisoner.
Come in. Get lost. This is our home from home.

8: The Cottage That Wasn't

My level best was never good enough
and when you took your leave, you left me in.
Our low-slung shell was filled with pleasure stuff
you thought the good went bad, felt put upon.

This place was thatched to order, plastered well
with tacky, pink-washed views for sundry souls.
We wanted that: you gasped for more, until
the chintzy thrills - camellia prints - got spilt.

And how I wish that imprint might have fused
appended by our photographs, your clothes.
Our homes are little more than wardrobes: lose
a simple suit like love, and wear untruths.

I'm not at home *chez moi*. But neighbours see
the better guy your leaving leaves me with.

Distant Close

6: Rocky

After strangely-dangerous days evaporated
there came a cold explosion. What was a marriage
hung like sun-dust in those rooms, where loving rose.
The wreckage was oddly ordered, files and features
ranged across a landing, toppling into waves
like portraits peering up a straitened stairwell.

What they had craved framed him becoming her
their puzzle weirdly-wicked had it only
as a kink in where their families touched,
a glimpse of farce within those poorer walls.
He missed the urgent undertows of loneliness;
she missed emerging shoals, as bright as glass.

And dangerously-strange ways coagulated
and no one noticed anyone trapped, or free.

4: Withdraw and Fade

When did that irresistible trigger bust itself,
in some duff second of our dull routines?
You'd been sharp, well-graded, better groomed
and mainly there with a chance of catching the main eye.

There'd always been a cranky street that you'd longed
to migrate to, or batty catalogues of fashions
and the bother of bothering about who would wear
what, and where, and why. And how it cost.

For the largest percentage of everyone, the safest bet,
becomes that unlikely chance of being lucky and safe,
measures the adventures you've had: a hundred plans,
a couple of dozen dreams - some bungalow-binge.

2: Coldfish

Up-ended ceiling, pewter mirror, superficial
and taut, like membranes
of imagined cauls.

Polythene part: pendulous, plastic, globular
and eras of peering through semi-algae.
Childhood dries.

Variant daylight, bleared and luminous planes of glass
shatter late, submerge early,
no *brightyoungthing*.

Some weekend schemes through these poor walls
blown, bombarded by clamour,
roaming home, hurt.

Pebbles in re-filtered water, shingle-minded
cubed lagoons of languidness,
just alive, alone.

Will Daunt

REVIEWS

HOUSES DIM (2000)

Strange ways of life are presented as normality ...It's an excellent, though disturbing collection.
N.H.I. REVIEW

These are concise, veiled poems ... One of the things I particularly like is the masterly control of both adjectives, and of ... images and metaphors ... As a poem should hold, refreshment of language.
Anne Born in LINKS 9

Now this is about real landscapes. Descriptions so gripping they'll have you turning your collar up in your own front room... Good one.
KRAX 38

2000 TALES OF LOVE, REWINDING (2001)

... set to a diary of dates; tales of travel and stillness, from forgotten names to millennium eve in the poet's deadpan but clever language.
The Affectionate Punch

LANCASHIRE WORKING (2003)

This collection of poems could well have been called A Book of Forms such is the scope and craftsmanship of Will Daunt's work. This collection is ultimately worth the graft of the reader. Will Daunt is building a fine body of work, one that warrants a more comprehensive collection sooner rather than later.
John G. Hall, N.H.I. REVIEW

Deals with place and time, sometimes writes eloquently and at other times, raw and straight to the point. Interesting use of language of imagery. I enjoyed this collection.
Alice Lenkiewicz, in NEON HIGHWAY 8

RUNNING OUT OF ENGLAND (2004)

There is an economy of language that mirrors both the harsh landscapes and the personal tragedies. LOST ONE is a bleak moving sequence on a still birth, where the accumulation of technical words — from the freeze-frame, scanner, disconnecting, plug, of the first two poems contrast with the bleakness of the aftermath —

> nothing beyond the empty branch,
> and a child without a brother,
> the silence.

Daunt is at home with many different verse forms and is a remarkable wordsmith.
Jacqueline Karp in N.H.I. ONLINE

THE GOOD IS ABROAD (2006)

In *The Good is Abroad* Will Daunt moves from subject to subject and from situation to situation with effortless ease; and with each movement he presents us with a handful of nuggets which, though melancholy, shine in splendour. Firmly ensconced in his existence, supremely confident of his own being, the poet looks around, as if bewildered, by the very objects and situations that define his identity.
John Pilgrim (THE QUILL AND INK)

...he's at his special best on landscape, on place and mood and the shifting moment, for instance in the quartet of poems with compass bearings ... Here the pattern of tight rhymes repeated induces its own elegiac tone. The same is true of *Island Lines*, four short poems which have their own individual kinds of quiet resonance; or the terse, accurate *In The Ruff* ...where deep affection lies behind the lines. *Channel Railways* similarly illustrates the precision of his vision.
R.V. BAILEY IN ENVOI 144

This collection gives bleakness and alienation a rhythmic thrust that leaves a reader more breathless than bereft. Good writing transmits energy from its creator to the page; and Mr Daunt is a dynamo. Throughout the collection there is palpable immediacy — and nowhere is it more apparent than in SPEAK TO ME ... a perfect example of that edgy style.
MICHAEL BANGERTER, N.H.I. ONLINE REVIEW

To be a good poet you need to be an observer of life and nature. To be a very good poet you need to be an observer with empathy. Will Daunt in his latest collection 'The Good is Abroad' seems to demonstrate that he has both these qualities. And perhaps even a bit more; he likes to play tricks with words.
JOHN PLEVIN, PULSAR MARCH 2007

There's that final five minute view of the hills or the sea when you're tired and heading off to bed - a feeling that wipes out you immediate companions, the hoi polloi and the traffic - just you and the chill of evening. That is what Will captures best in his writing ... this book belongs as bedside reading in the camper van, canalboat, or overnight lodge. A couple of witty pieces near the end remind us we're in the real world and to snap out of the dream - but you might not want to.
KRAX 44

Distant Close